ChatGPT Prompts Book

ChatGPT Prompts Book

Precision Prompts, Priming, Training & AI Writing Techniques for Mortals

Oliver Theobald

Scatterplot Press LTD

CONTENTS

FOREWORD

I didn't want to write this book. Despite writing about AI since 2015, it wasn't my place to onboard users onto a new platform with the fastest rate of adoption in human history. I also had another important reason to avoid ChatGPT.

In *Machine Learning for Absolute Beginners: A Plain English Introduction*, I echoed the prediction of the time that AI would soon replace low-skill labor through automation, self-driving vehicles, and robotics. In a cruel but ironic twist of fate, AI is now overtaking me with its rapid writing capabilities and deep knowledge of virtually everything.

Within a week of ChatGPT's launch, Amazon.com was filled with various ultimate guides to ChatGPT, authored by ChatGPT and uploaded by people early to the opportunity.

I was skeptical. How could you fill a book on the topic of a software program with no code, no hotkeys, no parameters, and a user interface with barely any buttons?

I had played with ChatGPT and while its writing syntax and speed were impressive, it lacked the precision of a human writer and the discipline to stay on topic. Over the next two weeks, I took the time to observe, understand, and think about the limitations of the model. With this knowledge, I was able to develop strategies to overcome the inefficiencies and focus on leveraging ChatGPT's strengths to achieve improved results. Using these strategies, I soon found myself using ChatGPT daily and I upgraded to the Pro subscription.

While I was finding ways to streamline my day job using ChatGPT for translation and small writing tasks, I assumed everyone else was using ChatGPT to work more efficiently too. But time and again, I heard colleagues and friends lamenting the quality of the outputs the AI model was generating. They were using ChatGPT as a search tool to extract information from the Internet or overloading the model with complex tasks and minimal instructions. They were running into the same problems I encountered when I started using ChatGPT.

Part of the problem was the open-ended nature of the software and the lack of scenario-specific modules or features. Unlike other AI writing software, ChatGPT has no special features for writing social media titles or blog posts—just a big blank canvas.

I found collections of AI text prompts online, but I was frustrated by the absence of strategy and guiding principles; I was eager to understand the qualities that make a text prompt effective.

Around this time, I had just finished writing a book on *Generative AI Art for Beginners*, which involved studying the topic of text prompts. Through this process, I gained a deeper understanding of how to craft an effective prompt to generate images and art using DALL-E (ChatGPT's artistic sibling) and other AI art services.

Realizing that others could also benefit from this knowledge, I decided to share my findings by writing this short book on the topic of text prompts for ChatGPT.

In this book, I aim to provide a clear and concise playbook outlining the best practices for creating text prompts for ChatGPT. As a summary of my findings over the last four months, I hope this book serves you well in harnessing the full potential of ChatGPT and surviving in a fast-changing world!Bottom of Form

1

INTRODUCTION

In a complex world, language is the ultimate tool for human interaction and cooperation. From the earliest grunts and gestures to revolutionary manifestos and evocative Tweetstorms, language allows us to share ideas, express emotions, and build connections with one another. However, as our communication needs have evolved, so too has the technology that underpins it. Today, we have new language tools that are transforming the way we communicate and generate ideas. From customer service chatbots to personal assistants, these new tools are making it possible for machines to interact with humans in a natural manner.

Leading the way is ChatGPT, an AI language model developed by OpenAI. Founded by Sam Altman in 2015, OpenAI is the same company behind DALL-E, an innovative new AI art tool for generating art and images in seconds.

The release of ChatGPT has now solidified OpenAI's brand on a global scale. With its advanced natural language processing (NLP) capabilities, ChatGPT can understand and respond to human language in a way that was once thought impossible. From simple text prompts to complex documentation, ChatGPT is capable of analyzing the context of a conversation and generating responses that are not only coherent and relevant but also applicable to real-world communication.

But the question remains whether ChatGPT is a futuristic gimmick or a practical solution for increasing productivity. Is this the new way of writing? What are the risks? Can I outsource my job to ChatGPT?

In this book, we will discuss the technology behind ChatGPT, its capabilities and limitations, and how to get the best out of this powerful new tool. We will also explore the rules of ChatGPT, including advanced text prompts, use cases, and its potential to revolutionize the way you work.

Whether you are a writer, a linguist, a student, a knowledge worker, or simply someone interested in the future of communication, this book has something to offer. So, come along on this journey, and let's explore the future of AI-powered communication.

2

UNVEILING CHATGPT

The development of ChatGPT represents a significant milestone in the ongoing quest for advanced language models. By combining the power of machine learning and natural language processing, ChatGPT can generate contextually relevant and coherent text, opening up a world of possibilities across different industries and applications. From simulating conversations and generating content to answering questions and summarizing text, ChatGPT's versatility is transforming the way we interact with and harness AI. As you delve deeper into the world of ChatGPT, you will uncover its immense potential and the limitless opportunities it presents. First, though, it's important to understand the core technology behind this ground-breaking application.

ChatGPT, short for Chat Generative Pre-trained Transformer, is based on the GPT-4 architecture. Without delving into the specific mechanics of the underlying architecture, it's important to have a base understanding of machine learning and natural language processing.

Machine learning refers to the process of teaching a model to recognize patterns, relationships, and structures within a dataset, enabling it to make predictions and generate coherent responses to user inputs. In the case of ChatGPT, the GPT model is trained to acquire the ability to understand and generate human-like text based on the vast amounts of data it has been trained on.

NLP is another subfield of artificial intelligence that overlaps with machine learning but deals with enabling computers to comprehend, interpret, and generate human language. By understanding the likelihood of words appearing together, NLP language models can be used for a wide array of applications, such as machine translation, speech recognition, and text generation.

In the case of ChatGPT, the model functions by predicting the most probable next word in a sequence based on the input from the user. This process is then repeated for each subsequent word, allowing it to generate coherent and contextually relevant sentences in the form of a chat conversation.

The model used for ChatGPT has been trained on vast amounts of publicly available data, known as the "WebText" dataset, which enables it to understand a wide range of topics and produce responses that mimic human-like text. The primary aim of the dataset was to provide the model with as much knowledge as possible by exposing it to various topics, writing styles, and perspectives.

A few of these data sources include:

1. **Websites:** ChatGPT was trained on content from millions of websites, including news articles and blog posts covering a wide array of topics, including science, technology, politics, history, and culture.
2. **Books:** The model was trained on excerpts from books, both fiction and non-fiction, to expose it to different writing styles, genres, and narrative structures.
3. **Online forums:** This includes content collected from online forums and discussion boards, such as Reddit and Stack Overflow, which provided ChatGPT with examples of informal language and conversation, as well as a variety of opinions and viewpoints.
4. **Social media:** Text from social media platforms, including Twitter and Facebook, was used to help ChatGPT understand shorter and more casual forms of text, including slang and abbreviations.

5. **Conversational data:** ChatGPT was trained on conversational data from customer support logs, public chat rooms, and other sources to improve its ability to engage in dialogue and understand the context in a conversational setting.

ChatGPT-4

At the time of writing, ChatGPT operates on the GPT-4 architecture, which is the latest version in a series of GPT models and the culmination of decades of research and innovation in language modeling.

For context, the earliest language models were primarily statistical, relying on frequency counts of words and word sequences in large corpora (database containing text) to estimate probabilities. While these models helped to lay the groundwork for understanding language, they were limited in their ability to capture the complex relationships and context that define human language.

With the advent of neural networks and deep learning, a new generation of language models emerged. These models, known as recurrent neural networks (RNNs) and long short-term memory (LSTM) networks, were better equipped to handle the sequential nature of language, allowing for improved predictions and more sophisticated text generation.

GPT, developed by OpenAI, has since marked a significant advancement in the evolution of language models. The first GPT model, released in 2018, introduced a novel approach to pre-training and fine-tuning, setting the stage for more powerful and versatile language models.

GPT-2, released in 2019, subsequently built upon the success of its predecessor, demonstrating even greater capabilities in generating coherent and contextually relevant text. Despite its impressive performance, GPT-2 still faced numerous limitations, including difficulties with handling longer text sequences and the generation of nonsensical or inaccurate responses.

The release of GPT-3 in 2020 marked a new era for language models, showcasing unprecedented performance and versatility. The success of GPT paved the way for the popular ChatGPT application built upon the GPT-4 architecture.

GPT-4 utilizes a deep learning technique known as the Transformer, which has become the cornerstone of many state-of-the-art NLP models. This enables ChatGPT to effectively process and generate text, accounting for context and relationships between words and phrases with higher accuracy. This allows it to generate highly context-aware and human-like text, addressing many of the shortcomings of earlier models.

Use Cases

Unlike traditional pre-programmed software, which typically has a well-defined set of features and use cases, ChatGPT offers a more flexible and adaptable approach to handling tasks. It can be used for a wide range of potential purposes and this versatility sets it apart from conventional software, making it a valuable tool for various tasks and industries.

Additionally, as the technology behind ChatGPT evolves, it will continue to improve in terms of accuracy, relevance, and overall performance. With the right instructions, known as a "text prompt" (and a skill we'll cover in the coming chapters), there really are limitless possibilities. Below is a brief list of some popular use cases.

1. **Conversation Simulation**
   ChatGPT can engage in conversations with users, simulating the experience of chatting with another human person. This can be particularly useful for customer support, virtual assistance, and education, including foreign language learning.
2. **Content Generation**
   ChatGPT can generate text content for articles, blog posts, and

other creative writing purposes, saving users time and effort, and making writer's block a thing of the past.

3. **Question-Answering**

   ChatGPT can provide answers to questions within its knowledge domain. While there are limitations to its knowledge, this can be useful for students, researchers, or anyone seeking information on a given topic.

4. **Idea Brainstorming**

   The software can help you to generate ideas or suggestions for projects, products, case studies, or other creative endeavors that you are working on.

5. **Text Summarization**

   ChatGPT can summarize long pieces of text, providing concise overviews of articles, reports, books, and examples of your own writing.

6. **Language Translation**

Although not specifically designed for translation, ChatGPT can assist with translating text between various languages, acting as a supplementary tool for language learners and translators.

Limitations of ChatGPT

While ChatGPT has made significant advances in natural language processing, it still has a number of limitations that users should be aware of when using this application.

In this section, we'll explore some of the key limitations of Chat-GPT, including its inability to reason or understand the context and the potential for biased responses. Note, however, that these limitations will be addressed and improved upon over time.

Time Relevant Information

As an AI language model, ChatGPT does not search the Internet in real-time and is not even connected to the Internet. As an AI language model, ChatGPT was exposed to knowledge from an extensive repository of text and language data, gathered from sources such as books, articles, and websites. This means that its knowledge is limited to a finite amount of sources as well as the time at which the data was collected. At the time of writing, ChatGPT-3 and ChatGPT-4 are only trained on data collected up to and before September 2021. As a result, the model might not be aware of events, developments, or trends that occurred after 2021.

To demonstrate this limitation, if we ask ChatGPT about the Silicon Valley Bank crisis unfolding in early 2023, the model is unable to generate a credible and up-to-date response to our request. As the model explains, new information has emerged since its knowledge cutoff (the period when it was initially trained).

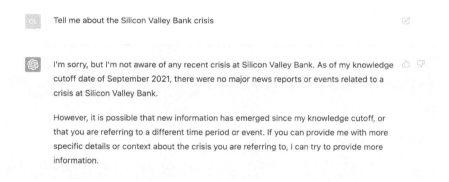

It's therefore essential to keep an eye out for updates regarding ChatGPT's most recent knowledge cutoff date, and alternatively explore other software applications with a more recent cutoff date or access to live knowledge if you wish to generate content based on recent events. If you are a fiction author or a 20th Century history teacher, then obviously, you won't have to worry as much about ChatGPT's latest cutoff date.

Inability to Reason

The next limitation of ChatGPT is its inability to reason like a human. While it can quickly generate responses based on patterns it has learned from the training data (the dataset used to train the model), it lacks the ability to understand the underlying concepts or make logical deductions. This means that it may struggle to answer complex questions that require critical thinking or problem-solving.

For example, if you ask ChatGPT **What is the meaning of life?**, it may provide a generic response based on the patterns it has learned, rather than understanding the logical reasoning behind someone asking this question.

Biased Responses

As a new technology, the extent and nature of bias associated with AI model design have yet to be fully documented. Although the capabilities of ChatGPT are impressive, they may also reflect and exaggerate societal biases. Given that ChatGPT is mostly trained on data crawled from the Internet, it can generate content that contains or purports harmful stereotypes. This means that if the training data is skewed towards a particular demographic, political, or geographical location, ChatGPT's responses may reflect that bias. For example, if the training data is biased towards male viewpoints on a certain topic, ChatGPT may struggle to generate accurate responses to female viewpoints on that topic. This is because it has learned patterns from biased data and may not have enough information to generate accurate responses for a particular demographic of people.

Commoditization of Content

While ChatGPT can generate high-quality content, it is important to note that the output is based on patterns it has learned from the training data. Therefore, with multiple users generating content using the same training data, the content will be affected by fewer individual perspectives, especially for generic prompts such as **Write a blog about X.**

It's possible that the widespread use of ChatGPT to generate content may also lead to some level of commoditization in the content space, with many blogs and other forms of content middling on the same arguments, language, case studies, and facts.

Emotional Intelligence

ChatGPT does not have emotional intelligence like humans. It cannot understand or empathize with emotions, which limits its ability to provide emotional support or advice. This means that it may provide generic or irrelevant responses when dealing with emotional issues.

For example, if you ask ChatGPT for advice on dealing with anxiety, it may provide a generic response based on the patterns it has learned, rather than understanding the specific emotional state that you are in.

Informational Errors

AI language models remain a work in progress and ChatGPT does make mistakes, including incomplete, incorrect, or outdated information. ChatGPT's responses may also include references to case studies or other sources of information that aren't accessible through a simple Google search and raises the question of trust and transparency. This means you should be wary of relying on ChatGPT's responses as a sole source of information, especially when it comes to making important decisions or drawing conclusions.

It's also critical to fact-check the information that ChatGPT produces and ask ChatGPT for links to any case studies or research reports that it mentions (in order to check whether they actually exist).

The Future Development of ChatGPT

As with all technologies, ChatGPT and the evolution of language models are bound to develop, with each new iteration building upon the successes and lessons learned from previous models. Future advancements may include better handling of context and ambiguities, improved understanding of idiomatic expressions and figurative language, and more robust reasoning abilities, which will bring significant improvements for us as users.

In this section, we'll explore some of the possible future developments of ChatGPT and other AI language models, including improved contextual understanding, emotional intelligence, and creativity.

1. ***Improved Contextual Understanding:*** One of the main areas of development for ChatGPT and other AI language models is improved contextual understanding. Current models are limited in their ability to understand the context of a conversation, which can lead to irrelevant or incorrect responses. Future developments are likely to focus on improving the models' ability to understand the nuances of a conversation and grasp the intent behind the words. For example, future models may be able to understand the tone and emotions of a conversation, allowing for more accurate responses. This would be particularly useful in situations such as customer service, where understanding the customer's emotions is crucial.

2. ***Emotional Intelligence:*** Another area of development for ChatGPT and other AI language models is emotional intelligence. While current models lack emotional intelligence, future developments may enable the models to understand and empathize with emotions, allowing for more accurate and personalized responses. For example, future models may be able to recognize when a customer is angry or upset and provide appropriate responses that acknowledge their emotions. This would be particularly useful in situations such as crisis management, where providing emotional support is critical.

3. ***Creativity:*** Current AI language models such as ChatGPT can generate original responses, but they lack the creativity and

imagination of humans. Future developments may focus on improving the models' creativity, allowing them to generate more original and unique ideas. For instance, future models may be able to generate more diverse and imaginative responses to creative writing prompts, allowing for more engaging and compelling content creation.

4. *Multilingual Capabilities:* Another area of development for ChatGPT and other AI language models is multilingual capabilities. While current models can generate responses in multiple languages, they may struggle with idiomatic expressions and other nuances that are specific to a particular language or culture. Future developments may focus on improving the model's ability to understand and generate responses in multiple languages, including regional dialects and slang. This would be particularly useful in situations such as language translation and cross-cultural communication.

In conclusion, the future developments of ChatGPT and other AI language models are likely to bring significant improvements in contextual understanding, emotional intelligence, creativity, and multilingual capabilities. These developments will make AI language models even more powerful tools for communication and problem-solving in a wide range of settings.

3

GETTING STARTED WITH CHATGPT

Now that you have a basic understanding of what ChatGPT is and what it can be used for, it's time to explore this technology further. In the next chapter, we'll dive into the practical aspects of interacting with ChatGPT.

To begin using ChatGPT, you will need to first visit the OpenAI website (www.openai.com) and navigate to their signup page for Chat-GPT. Next, fill in the required information, including your name, email address, and password, and then complete the registration process by following the instructions sent to your email account.

ChatGPT currently offers a free and paid version. As these versions are subject to change in regard to their features and pricing, I will not delve into the specifics of each option. For first-time users, I recommend using the freemium version (if it is available) and continue using it until you feel comfortable with the level of service provided and the value you are gaining from the service.

If you encounter any problems with slow processing speed or identify benefits included in the paid version that apply to your needs, then you can consider upgrading to the paid version as an individual user or as an enterprise user on behalf of your employer/company. Personally, I currently use ChatGPT Plus for USD $20 a month as this gives me access to ChatGPT-4 as well as faster processing speed and higher availability, which helps me get my work done faster.

With that said, let's get started!

Interacting with ChatGPT doesn't require any specialized programming or AI knowledge. With the right attitude and guidance, anyone can become a master of ChatGPT. That said, constructing a good prompt requires practical experience, including knowledge of ChatGPT's strengths and limitations. This is a skill you can easily develop through experimentation and by applying some of the tips and strategies covered in this book.

After setting up an account with OpenAI and logging into Chat-GPT, you can click on the "+ **New chat**" button in the top-left corner of the landing page or simply type your instructions into the chat bar on the right-hand side.

Figure 1: ChatGPT's simple user interface

Chats

Located on the left-hand side of the screen, you will see a history of your chats automatically saved to your account. This lets you easily access past conversations and refer back to your text prompts and other important information.

This feature also enables you to organize multiple projects into designated chats. This allows for a more streamlined and efficient workflow as users can easily switch between projects and access relevant information without having to search through a single chat history.

It is also important to separate your ChatGPT chats based on topics to avoid confusing the AI language model. ChatGPT uses a deep learning algorithm that relies on context to generate responses, so if the conversation jumps between different topics or contexts, it may not be able to generate the most coherent or relevant responses.

By keeping each ChatGPT chat focused on a specific topic, you can help the AI language model to better understand the context of the conversation and generate more accurate responses.

Text Prompts

To interact with ChatGPT, you will need to provide what's called a *text prompt*, which is instructions for the AI about what you wish to generate. A prompt can be as simple as **What is ChatGPT?** or **Translate your previous output in French**. ChatGPT will then do its best to generate an output based on the text prompt provided.

 What is ChatGPT?

 ChatGPT is an AI language model developed by OpenAI based on the GPT architecture. It is designed to understand and generate human-like text, enabling it to engage in conversations, answer questions, and provide information on a wide range of topics. ChatGPT's capabilities make it a useful tool for various applications, from content creation to virtual assistance.

There is no single method or specific code for writing a text prompt. There are no special or specific keywords that ChatGPT is programmed to respond to exclusively. You can ask ChatGPT any question or provide any input, and ChatGPT will do its best to generate a relevant response.

While it's possible to generate high-quality outputs using a sentence fragment (i.e. **blog post about personal finance**), you will generally get more relevant results using an imperative (i.e. **draft a blog post about personal finance**), a full sentence (i.e. **A blog post about personal finance**), or multiple sentences (i.e. **Draft a blog post about personal finance. The blog should include sections on credit card management and savings hacks**).

It is vital to use natural language as that's the language the AI is trained on. Natural language refers to human languages, such as everyday conversational English or what you might write in a text message, as opposed to an artificial language such as a programming language. This means you should communicate to ChatGPT like it's a human and avoid using artificial languages such as CSS, Python, or Google search parameters to write your text prompts. You can also use other natural languages such as French, Spanish, Japanese, etc.

Next, although there are no set rules for interacting with ChatGPT, you should take the following tips into consideration.

Use proper grammar and punctuation: ChatGPT is programmed to understand and respond to proper grammar and punctuation. If you use improper grammar or punctuation, ChatGPT may not be able to understand your question or may provide an inadequate response.

Try open-ended questions: Open-ended questions allow ChatGPT to generate more detailed and informative responses. For example, instead of asking **Do you like cats?**, try asking **What is your opinion on dogs as pets?**

Try to use verbs: Using verbs can be helpful in giving ChatGPT a clearer understanding of what you are asking or telling it to do. Verbs are action words that convey a specific meaning, and by using them, you indicate to ChatGPT what action you want it to take or what type of response you are looking for. Examples of verbs include *write, answer,* *translate, optimize, calculate, explain,* etc. However, it's important to remember that ChatGPT is a language model, and it can understand and respond to a wide range of inputs, including prompts without any verbs. So, while using verbs can be helpful, it's not always necessary for ChatGPT to understand your request or generate a relevant response.

Use quotation marks: Using quotation marks can sometimes be helpful to separate the command from the subject matter. An example of this would be using quotation marks to highlight the phrase you wish to translate or summarize, i.e. **Translate "apple" into French.**

Don't be afraid to correct ChatGPT: If ChatGPT provides an incorrect or inappropriate response, don't be afraid to correct it. This helps improve ChatGPT's performance and ensures that you receive more accurate responses in the future. You can leave feedback by clicking on the thumbs-up and thumbs-down arrows on the right-hand side of the arrow or by directly correcting ChatGPT in your follow-up message. (Regenerating the outcome is also an indirect way to leave feedback.)

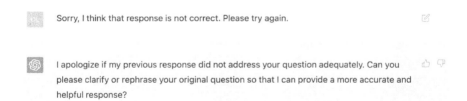

Sorry, I think that response is not correct. Please try again.

I apologize if my previous response did not address your question adequately. Can you please clarify or rephrase your original question so that I can provide a more accurate and helpful response?

Provide more context: If you are not happy with ChatGPT's output, this is usually a sign that the model needs more information or context to help it generate an accurate and relevant response.

Rephrase your message: Another way to improve the output is to try to rephrase your original input in a different way. ChatGPT is a language model that generates responses based on the input it receives, so by rephrasing your question or input, you might be able to get a different and more satisfactory response.

Sample ChatGPT Prompts

Below are some sample text prompts you can use to experiment with using ChatGPT.

Tell me a joke about ____
Yep, ChatGPT is capable of generating humorous responses!

What book/movie/song should I read/watch/listen to next? I also like ____. Give me recommendations based on that.
ChatGPT can provide you with recommendations on books, movies, and music based on your interests.

Can you help me with [math/grammar/science] homework? I need help understanding ____
ChatGPT can provide you with explanations and solutions to various academic subjects.

What's the difference between ____ and ____?
Ask ChatGPT to answer simple questions about the difference between particular words (i.e. empathy and sympathy) or different topics (i.e. Christianity and Judaism).

I'm learning to speak ____. Please chat with me in ____ to help me practice.
Use ChatGPT to practice chatting in a new language such as Japanese, French, Italian, etc.

Tell me about ____.

You can ask ChatGPT to define any terms of theories you don't understand.

I'm writing a non-fiction book about ___ and I'm looking for an interesting scientific case study that explores the idea of ___ and ___. Please suggest some options.

ChatGPT can be an effective research assistant, but always make sure that you double-check the accuracy and reliability of any studies, information, or claims that it provides.

Hotkeys & Shortcuts

At present, ChatGPT does not have hotkeys or shortcuts that you can use to streamline your workflow. However, some chat platforms that integrate with ChatGPT may have their own keyboard shortcuts or commands that you can use to interact with the chat interface more efficiently.

For example, some platforms may allow you to use the Tab key to cycle through available response options or use the arrow keys to navigate through previous messages. Additionally, some platforms may offer commands that allow you to perform specific actions, such as generating or copying an output.

It's important to check the documentation or Help resources for the specific platform you are using to chat with ChatGPT to see if any hotkeys or shortcuts are available.

Privacy

As an AI language model, ChatGPT does not have a memory of past conversations with its users or the capability to store that information. However, according to OpenAI, it does use machine learning to continually refine its responses based on user input. This means that when

ChatGPT sees a question or prompt that it has seen before, it may be able to generate a better response based on its previous interactions.

In summary, you shouldn't be concerned with ChatGPT disclosing your conversations with other users or public datasets, but keep in mind that it does observe your prompts and feedback (thumbs-up and thumbs-down button) or the frequency at which you regenerate a response in order to optimize the output.

Ownership

According to ChatGPT's Content Policy (labs.openai.com/policies/content-policy) and Terms (openai.com/policies/terms-of-use), you retain ownership of the content generated by ChatGPT. This includes the rights to republish, sell, and merchandise outputs, irrespective of whether they were produced using a free or paid subscription. This means that you use content generated by ChatGPT for personal and commercial projects as long as that content doesn't infringe on the copyright of existing content and the terms and conditions for publishing content on other platforms.

4

PRECISION PROMPT WRITING

Prompt construction is where you will see the difference between an average user and a power user. In general, the more specific your prompt is, the better ChatGPT can understand what you are asking, and the more specific your outcome will be. For instance, instead of asking a general question like **What is the meaning of life?**, try asking a more specific question like **What are the main philosophies on the meaning of life?**

In the previous chapter, we looked at the simple prompt in the form of **draft a blog post about personal finance** (using a verb at the start of the prompt to form an imperative[1]). While there is ample information here for ChatGPT to generate a relevant output, we can refine this prompt to generate a more nuanced and less generic output.

This is where *modifiers* come in. While your base prompt will generally describe the general task, a modifier adds additional instructions regarding the style, tone, or voice you want ChatGPT to use.

a blog post about personal finance written in the style of the Bible: King James version

Base prompt   **Modifier**

If we take the original base prompt of **a blog about personal finance,** we can add a modifier in the form of **a blog post about personal finance written in the style of the Bible: King James version.** Obviously, this will produce a dramatically different result from the original prompt.

Similarly, you could use a modifier to specify a particular style of writing based on a well-known author such as J.K. Rowling or Tim Ferriss.

Text Prompt:
Craft a blog post about personal finance written in the style of Tim Ferriss

 Craft a blog post about personal finance written in the style of Tim Ferriss

 Welcome to the Tim Ferriss Guide to Personal Finance. In this blog post, I'll share with you some of the strategies and tactics that have helped me and others I know to optimize our finances.

First and foremost, it's important to understand that personal finance isn't just about budgeting and saving money. It's about designing your life in a way that allows you to have the financial freedom to pursue your passions and goals.

Here are some tips and tricks that can help you achieve that:

1. Automate your finances

One of the easiest and most effective ways to optimize your personal finance is to automate it. Set up automatic bill payments, automatic savings transfers, and automatic investments. This not only ensures that you never miss a payment or contribution, but it also makes it easier to stick to your budget and avoid overspending.

2. Focus on the big wins

Additionally, you can also add multiple modifiers by stacking them together.

Text Prompt:

Draft a blog post about personal finance written in the style of the Bible: King James version, inclusive language, U.S. spelling.

 Draft a blog post about personal finance written in the style of the Bible: King James version, inclusive language, U.S. spelling.

 Title: The Book of Wealth: A Testament to Financial Wisdom in the Style of the King James Bible

1. In the beginning, the Lord did bless the children of the earth with the bounty of the land, that they may partake of its fruits and rejoice in its abundance.
2. And behold, there came a time when the children of the earth were called upon to manage their treasures and to provide for their households, that they may live in prosperity and peace.
3. Thus, the Lord spake unto them, saying, "Verily, I say unto thee, be thou wise stewards of the riches I have bestowed upon thee."
4. And so, the children of the earth did seek knowledge and understanding in matters of coin, that they might be found faithful in their stewardship.
5. First, the Lord commanded the children of the earth to prepare a plan for their sustenance, that they might know the measure of their abundance and the portion which they must render unto the Lord.
6. And the Lord spake, saying, "Make thee a budget, for by it shalt thou know the measure of thine income and the extent of thine expenditures, and with this

Here, we added two new modifiers: **inclusive language** and **U.S. spelling**. However, if you find yourself using the same modifiers with multiple text prompts, then you may like to request ChatGPT to use these modifiers for all future outputs within that chat thread.

Text Prompt:
Please always use U.S. spelling and inclusive language for all outputs in this chat thread.

> Please always use U.S. spelling and inclusive language for all outputs in this chat thread.

> I apologize for any inconsistencies in my previous response. I will ensure that I use U.S. spelling and inclusive language in all outputs for this chat thread. If you have any further questions or require assistance, please feel free to ask.

After adding this information regarding style, you will no longer need to include those common modifiers for each text prompt. Alternatively, if you are working for a brand or company and you have fixed content guidelines regarding your organization's tone and voice, you can copy and paste those guidelines into the chat before you start producing content.

Text Prompt:
Please use the following tone and voice when generating outputs in this chat:

- **Use active voice, avoid passive voice**
- **Avoid slang and jargon, write in plain English**
- **Write positively, use positive language rather than negative language**

Above is an example of Mailchimp's (an email marketing service company) writing style tips that feed into all their online content.

While it's possible to copy and paste internal content guidelines into ChatGPT, it's worthwhile investing time to create a special ChatGPT prompt that clearly summarizes your content guidelines. This way, ChatGPT can better understand your content requirements and other team members can use the same prompt for their own writing tasks.

Alternatively, you could ask ChatGPT to design writing style guidelines for your content based on your target audience, industry, and personality, for instance.

Text Prompt:

Please write content writing guidelines for a web3 company whose audience is web3 developers based predominately in the U.S., including tone and voice, spelling, and inclusive language. The guidelines should be short and sweet because they will be used as a text prompt for working with ChatGPT.

 Content Writing Guidelines for Web3 Company

1. Tone and Voice:
   - Maintain a professional yet approachable tone.
   - Use clear, concise language that is easy to understand.
   - Speak directly to web3 developers, addressing their needs and interests.
   - Employ a conversational style to encourage engagement and discussion.
2. Spelling:
   - Utilize U.S. spelling conventions for all content.
   - Double-check for spelling errors and typos before publishing.
3. Inclusive Language:
   - Be mindful of diversity and inclusivity in your writing.
   - Avoid language that may be perceived as discriminatory, biased, or offensive.
   - Use gender-neutral terms and pronouns when referring to individuals or groups.
   - Respect cultural differences and strive to represent a wide range of perspectives.

As seen in the screenshot, ChatGPT was able to generate writing guidelines based on our fictional company's needs. Note that you will need to verify and potentially edit the guidelines before putting them into action!

As demonstrated in this section, there any many ways to craft a text prompt and using modifiers is an effective method to avoid generic outputs and contributing to the online proliferation of content commoditization.

Maybe I Don't Want to be Specific!

While this chapter has spoken to the benefits of precise prompt writing, and incorporated multiple modifiers, it is also possible to go the opposite direction and let ChatGPT guide the conversation. Hence, rather than crafting a highly detailed prompt, you can use a vaguely defined prompt, such as **Blog about the future of the world**, and see what direction ChatGPT follows. This technique can be useful when you're still exploring content ideas and you aren't sure what exactly you want to write.

Likewise, you can use ChatGPT as an idea-generation tool by explaining your content goals and asking it for feedback.

Text Prompt:

I need to write a personal finance blog for Gen Z readers but I need help creating a structure and theme for this blog. Please generate 10 different paths I can take with this blog post.

 I need to write a personal finance blog for Gen Z readers but I need help creating a structure and theme for this blog. Please generate 10 different paths I can take with this blog post.

 Sure, here are 10 different paths you can take with your personal finance blog for Gen Z readers:

1. "Financial Planning for Gen Z: How to Start Building Your Wealth in Your 20s"
2. "Avoiding Common Money Mistakes: A Beginner's Guide to Personal Finance"
3. "Money-Saving Tips for College Students: How to Budget and Still Have Fun"
4. "The Pros and Cons of Investing in Cryptocurrencies: Is It Right for You?"
5. "How to Pay Off Your Student Loans Faster: Tips and Tricks"
6. "The Gig Economy: Making Money on Your Own Terms"
7. "The Importance of Building Good Credit and How to Do It"
8. "Investing in Your Future: How to Save for Retirement as a Gen Zer"
9. "The Ultimate Guide to Financial Independence and Retiring Early"
10. "Breaking Down the Gender Pay Gap: How to Negotiate Your Salary and Close the Gap".

As seen in the screenshot above, you can leverage ChatGPT to generate ideas and supplement the writing process, rather than relying solely on the model to generate the final content.

Negative Prompting

Negative prompting is a technique used to guide the AI toward generating an output while explicitly avoiding certain undesired information, words, or perspectives. By specifying what not to include in the answer, you can achieve a more focused and relevant output.

Negative prompting works by simply telling the model what not to include in its answer using words such as **avoid, do not, excluding**, etc.

Text Prompt:
Write a personal finance blog for Gen Z readers but avoid mentioning obvious strategies such as reducing expenses or high-risk strategies.

Text Prompt:
Tell me about different types of renewable energy sources, excluding solar power.

Overriding

All AI-trained models come with their own signature style. In the AI art field, AI models such as Midjourney and Craiyon lean toward more abstract and surrealist designs, whereas DALL-E 2 is better for generating realistic art and images.

In the case of ChatGPT, the default model tends to be overly wordy or verbose; ChatGPT will rarely give you a one-line answer. This issue stems from biases in how the model was trained, with the developers favoring lengthier and more comprehensive-looking answers. This makes sense, as this approach gives the model a higher chance of providing the user with at least something of use or relevant.

While longer answers can be useful by offering more options, interacting with ChatGPT over multiple messages can consume a longer amount of time than needed. If you wish to override or offset the default settings, you can use negative prompting (i.e. **don't organize**

information into dot points) or add a direct command to keep responses short, using words such as **quickly summarize, answer in one line, limit your response to 100 words,** etc.

Text Prompt:
Quickly tell me how many calories are in a banana

Quickly tell me how many calories in a banana

A medium-sized banana contains approximately 105 calories.

Another way to override the default settings is to dictate the format of the output. Rather than outputting information organized into dot pots, which is common, you can use negative prompting to stop ChatGPT from using this style of formatting, which could be useful for authors, for example.

Text Prompt:
Write a book chapter about _____ in the style of _____ without using dot points to organize information
Lastly, ChatGPT is typically coy or cautious about answering questions related to health, investing, and other potentially sensitive topics.

5

CONTENT WRITING

In today's digital age, content writing is a vital skill for businesses, educators, and individuals alike, and using ChatGPT to write content can be a highly productive and time-saving process.

This chapter will delve into the practical application of producing an engaging blog post and provide step-by-step guidance on harnessing ChatGPT for your own content creation pipeline. Additionally, you can also utilize these same techniques to create content for other mediums including newsletter content, podcast scripts, website content, social media copy, etc.

Step 1: Start a new chat

To avoid mixing topics and projects, it's important to create a new chat each time you start a new task.

Step 2: Brief ChatGPT on the task

Before tasking ChatGPT with writing an opening headline or the body of the blog, it helps to warm up the model with some background information about your blog. This can include information about the target audience, why you are writing this blog, and what are your goals. By providing this information up-front, ChatGPT will absorb this information as reference material for producing its outputs.

Text Prompt:

I want to write a blog post about looksmaxxing. I am writing this blog post on behalf of a male grooming company that specializes in shaving devices designed for men. My target audience is men aged between 15 and 40 years old who aren't regular customers of male grooming products and lack knowledge about the importance of personal grooming.

After inputting this background information, ChatGPT may add a comment congratulating you on your intention to write a blog post about the given topic or it might even jump to writing the blog content. Whatever the output, you can generally ignore it and proceed to Step 3.

Step 3: Choose your topic

Determine the subject of your blog post. Make sure it's specific and well-defined to get the most relevant content from ChatGPT. If you need help defining the topic, you can ask for help by asking ChatGPT for suggestions. As a tip, it usually helps to request multiple suggestions (using a number in your prompt) to avoid ChatGPT responding with one idea.

Text Prompt:
Generate 10 different blog topics about looksmaxxing

Generate 10 different blog topics about looksmaxxing

1. The Science of Attraction: Understanding How Looksmaxxing Boosts Your Confidence and Appeal
2. A Comprehensive Guide to Skincare for Men: How to Achieve a Flawless Complexion through Looksmaxxing
3. Dress to Impress: How to Revamp Your Wardrobe for the Ultimate Looksmaxxing Transformation
4. The Perfect Workout Routine for Looksmaxxing: Tips on Fitness and Nutrition for a Sculpted Physique
5. Hairstyles to Maximize Your Look: A Guide to Choosing the Perfect Cut for Your Face Shape and Hair Type
6. The Art of Manscaping: A Comprehensive Guide to Body Hair Grooming for Men
7. Elevate Your Scent Game: How to Choose the Right Fragrance for Your Personal Style and Body Chemistry
8. The Power of Posture: How to Improve Your Stance for a More Confident and Attractive Appearance
9. Boost Your Confidence with Dental Care: A Guide to Achieving a Brighter Smile and Fresher Breath
10. Looksmaxxing for the Busy Man: Quick and Easy Grooming Tips to Keep You Looking Sharp on the Go ↻ Regenerate response

Using ChatGPT as an idea-generation tool, we can either select one of its suggestions or use these suggestions to design our own topic. For this example, I want to use option 10, which is "Looksmaxxing for the Busy Man" as this topic fits well with the product I wish to promote.

Also, if you're wondering what *looksmaxxing* is, it's a trending term used online that refers to the process of maximizing one's physical appearance through various methods including grooming, exercise, diet, skincare, fashion, and even cosmetic procedures.

Step 4: Generate a headline

Now that we've selected a topic, we can either adopt this topic as the title or we can task ChatGPT to explore some even better options.

Text Prompt

Generate 10 headline alternatives for "Looksmaxxing for the Busy Man: Quick and Easy Grooming to Keep You Looking Sharp on the Go"

 Generate 10 headline alternatives for "Looksmaxxing for the Busy Man: Quick and Easy Grooming to Keep You Looking Sharp on the Go"

1. Stay Polished on the Move: Time-Saving Grooming Hacks for the Busy Modern Man
2. Grooming on the Fly: Effortless Looksmaxxing Tips for Men with Hectic Schedules
3. The Time-Pressed Man's Guide to Looking Sharp: Fast and Simple Grooming Techniques
4. No Time? No Problem! Speedy Grooming Tips for the Always-On-the-Go Man
5. Quick-Fix Grooming: How Busy Men Can Maintain a Polished Appearance with Minimal Effort
6. Groom and Zoom: Streamlined Looksmaxxing Strategies for Men in a Hurry
7. Mastering the Art of Fast Grooming: Time-Efficient Looksmaxxing Solutions for Today's Man
8. The 5-Minute Grooming Guide: Rapid Looksmaxxing Tips for Men with Busy Lives
9. Express Grooming: Time-Saving Looksmaxxing Techniques for Men on a Tight Schedule
10. The Rush Hour Groom: How to Maximize Your Look with Quick and Easy Grooming Tricks

Although option 8 would be a good option, I will stick with the original title as I want to place "Looksmaxxing" at the front of the title. Alternatively, I could go back and edit the text prompt to start the title with "Looksmaxxing."

Generate 10 headline alternatives for "Looksmaxxing for the Busy Man: Quick and Easy Grooming to Keep You Looking Sharp on the Go". The title should start with the keyword "Looksmaxxing"

1. Looksmaxxing on a Tight Schedule: Time-Saving Grooming Tips for the Modern Man
2. Looksmaxxing for Time-Strapped Gents: Fast and Efficient Grooming Hacks
3. Looksmaxxing in No Time: Streamlined Grooming Routines for Men on the Move
4. Looksmaxxing for Hectic Lives: Quick and Simple Grooming Tricks for Busy Men
5. Looksmaxxing Made Easy: Swift Grooming Techniques for the Man with Limited Time
6. Looksmaxxing for the Fast-Paced Lifestyle: Grooming Solutions for Men on the Go
7. Looksmaxxing in a Hurry: Rapid Grooming Strategies for the Busy Gentleman
8. Looksmaxxing for the Time-Conscious Man: Accelerated Grooming Tips to Stay Sharp
9. Looksmaxxing Express: Speedy Grooming Techniques for Men with Demanding Schedules
10. Looksmaxxing for the Active Man: No-Nonsense Grooming Tips for a Polished Appearance in Minutes

Step 5: Generate an outline

After selecting the title, let's generate an outline for the blog.

Text Prompt:

Generate an outline for the blog (Looksmaxxing for the Busy Man: Quick and Easy Grooming to Keep You Looking Sharp on the Go) with 5 sections. One section of the blog should cover the importance of male grooming and mention the product "Super Shaver" for all-purpose male grooming.

It's important to add the title of the blog so ChatGPT knows which title you decided to select. You can also add specific keywords or products that you want to mention within the blog.

Title: Looksmaxxing for the Busy Man: Quick and Easy Grooming to Keep You Looking Sharp on the Go

I. Introduction
A. Introduce the concept of looksmaxxing for busy men
B. Emphasize the importance of personal grooming in today's fast-paced world

II. The Importance of Male Grooming
A. Discuss the impact of grooming on self-confidence and first impressions
B. Mention the benefits of male grooming for overall health and hygiene
C. Highlight the "Super Shaver" as an all-purpose grooming tool for busy men

III. Quick and Efficient Shaving Techniques
A. Share time-saving shaving tips for men with busy schedules
B. Explain how the "Super Shaver" streamlines the grooming process
C. Offer advice for maintaining a clean, well-groomed appearance with minimal effort

IV. Time-Saving Hair and Skincare Hacks
A. Present easy hair care tips to keep your mane looking fresh and stylish
B. Provide recommendations for quick and effective skincare routines

V. Grooming on the Go: Strategies for Maintaining Your Look Throughout the Day
A. Offer solutions for quick touch-ups and grooming fixes when away from home
B. Suggest essential grooming items to keep in a travel kit or gym bag
C. Share strategies for incorporating grooming into a busy daily routine

VI. Conclusion
A. Recap the importance of looksmaxxing for busy men
B. Encourage readers to invest in their personal grooming and try the "Super Shaver" for efficient and effective results

Next, review the generated outline and refine it to suit your needs. For example, you may like to remove sections or switch up the sequence. You can do this manually by copying and pasting ChatGPT's outline into a Word Document and editing it there and then dropping the updated blog outline back into the chat. Alternatively, you can try to use text prompts to edit the outline within ChatGPT.

This approach works well if you only have one or two quick adjustments to make. If the outline needs major surgery, then it's generally worth taking some time to edit the outline using a text editor. Just remember to send the updated outline back to ChatGPT before you proceed to the next step.

Step 6: Write the blog

Using the selected outline, you can now start to write the blog. Here, we can either task ChatGPT to generate sections of the blog across multiple chat messages or we can try to write the full blog using a single text prompt. Also, don't forget to add modifiers to the prompt such as the style, tone, preferred spelling, target keywords, etc. In this example, I'll ask ChatGPT to mimic the writing style of James Clear, the author of *Atomic Habits: An Easy & Proven Way to Build Good Habits & Break Bad Ones*, and to use U.S. spelling.

Text Prompt:
Write the entire blog post based on the outline above in the style of James Clear using U.S English

If you're not satisfied with the output, you can try using the "**Regenerate response**" button (below the output) multiple times until you get an output that suits your needs. If this fails, you may need to go back and refine your original text prompt by clicking on the edit button.

Text Prompt:
Write the introduction of the blog post by expanding on the outline points above in the style of James Clear using U.S English

Write the entire blog post based on the outline above in the style of James Clear using U.S English

As a last resort, you can try slowing down the task by prompting ChatGPT to write the blog section by section, starting with the introduction and ending with the conclusion.

Step 7: Review and edit the content

While ChatGPT can be a valuable tool for content generation, it's essential to review and edit the output to ensure the final product is polished, accurate, and tailored to your target audience.

As you receive content for each section or for the full blog post, make sure that you review and edit it to ensure accuracy, clarity, and consistency. Check for grammatical errors, inconsistencies, and factual accuracy. Make any necessary edits to ensure the content flows and is engaging to readers. You might also like to use a third-party software such as Grammarly.com.

In general, poor spelling and grammar are far less of a problem compared to editing a draft written by a human writer. Instead, most of your time will be focused on fact-checking any statistics or claims mentioned in the content and checking that the content is relevant and on point.

If you are unhappy with individual sentences, you can copy and paste the sentence and request ChatGPT to re-write or optimize it.

Text Prompt:
optimize: But for the modern man, looking sharp and well-groomed is not only essential for making great first impressions; it also boosts self-confidence and contributes to overall well-being.

optimize: But for the modern man, looking sharp and well-groomed is not only essential for making great first impressions; it also boosts self-confidence and contributes to overall well-being.

For the modern man, not only is looking sharp and well-groomed crucial in making outstanding first impressions, but it also enhances self-confidence and promotes overall well-being.

Step 8: Optional extras

In the space of 10 minutes or so, you should have a convincing blog post at your disposal. Before you click publish, you may like to ask

ChatGPT to draft a metadata title and description for SEO purposes or a social media shout-out for a social channel such as LinkedIn or Facebook.

Text Prompt:
Write an SEO metadata description for the blog, optimized for Google

Write an SEO metadata description for the blog, optimized for Google

Discover time-saving grooming strategies for busy men, including shaving techniques, hair and skincare hacks, and on-the-go tips to keep you looking sharp. Elevate your grooming game with the "Super Shaver" and boost your confidence today.

Lastly, given that the current version of ChatGPT was only trained on data available before 2022, the language model will not be familiar with the latest social media and search engine optimization (SEO) strategies. To overcome this problem, you may need to manually train the model regarding new content writing strategies by inserting any relevant optimization rules into your text prompt.

A Word of Warning

While there's an obvious temptation to write an entire book, college essay, or SEO blog post using ChatGPT, it's important to use this software in combination with your own writing and editing. OpenAI is said to be developing cryptographic technology that can detect a signature in the words produced by OpenAI's text-generating AI models, with use cases for this technology including preventing students from using AI to complete their homework.

Amazon, Google, and other platforms are also wary of the impact that AI-generated content will have on the user experience for their users. As a result, they are likely to develop in-house tools to detect AI-generated content.

This is not to say that Google will penalize you for using ChatGPT to write the conclusion of your blog or that Amazon will prevent any use of AI writing tools in the production of self-published books. But there is a strong possibility that they and other major platforms will enforce a minimal threshold and request that a certain percentage of the content is original and not AI-generated.

To check the originality of content, you can use online services such as Originality.ai and Detect GPT that offer software tools for detecting AI-generated content and plagiarism.

ChatGPT Sample Blog

Below is the original version of the blog generated by ChatGPT-4, which is about 550 words in length and has not been edited by a human writer. While you could publish directly, the more time you spend on editing and updating the content—using either ChatGPT or a professional writer—the better the final piece.

Meta title: Quick Grooming Tips for Busy Men: Master Looksmaxxing & Stay Sharp On the Go

Meta description: For the modern man, not only is looking sharp and well-groomed crucial in making outstanding first impressions, but it also enhances self-confidence and promotes overall well-being.

Blog Title: Looksmaxxing for the Busy Man: Quick and Easy Grooming to Keep You Looking Sharp on the Go

Introduction:

In today's fast-paced world, personal grooming can feel like a luxury. But for the modern man, looking sharp and well-groomed is not only essential for making great first impressions; it also boosts self-confidence and contributes to overall well-being. The good news is that you don't have to sacrifice hours of your day to achieve a polished appearance. In this guide, we'll explore quick and easy grooming strategies for the busy man, including the benefits of using the "Super Shaver" to streamline your grooming routine.

The Importance of Male Grooming:

First impressions matter, and investing in your appearance pays dividends in both personal and professional settings. Grooming not only enhances your overall look but also helps you maintain good hygiene and feel more self-assured.

Enter the "Super Shaver," an all-purpose grooming tool designed for men who value both their time and appearance. With its versatile functionality and ease of use, the "Super Shaver" is the ideal solution for busy men looking to elevate their grooming game with minimal effort.

Quick and Efficient Shaving Techniques:

Shaving shouldn't be a chore or a time-consuming task. With the "Super Shaver," you can achieve a clean and well-groomed look in just a few minutes. Here are some tips to help you maximize efficiency:

Prep your skin: Before using the "Super Shaver," ensure your skin is clean and well-hydrated. This will make shaving smoother and more comfortable.

Use short, steady strokes: The "Super Shaver" is designed for precision, so let the device do the work. Avoid pressing too hard or making long strokes to reduce the risk of irritation.

Moisturize: After shaving, apply a soothing aftershave or moisturizer to keep your skin healthy and irritation-free.

Time-Saving Hair and Skincare Hacks:

When you're busy, it's easy to neglect your hair and skin. However, with a few simple tricks, you can maintain a fresh appearance without sacrificing precious time:

Choose a low-maintenance hairstyle: Opt for a haircut that requires minimal styling and is easy to manage.

Make the most of your shower: Use a 2-in-1 shampoo and conditioner to save time and streamline your hair care routine.

Opt for multi-purpose skincare products: Look for products that combine multiple benefits, such as a moisturizer with built-in SPF protection, to save time and keep your skin healthy.

Grooming on the Go: Strategies for Maintaining Your Look Throughout the Day:

No matter how busy your day gets, you can still maintain your polished appearance with these on-the-go grooming strategies:

Carry a compact grooming kit: Keep a small kit in your bag or car with essentials like a travel-sized "Super Shaver," toothbrush, toothpaste, comb, and facial wipes.

Make use of downtime: Take advantage of short breaks during the day to check your appearance and make quick touch-ups as needed.

Schedule regular grooming appointments: Prioritize self-care by setting reminders for regular haircuts and other grooming appointments to ensure you always look your best.

Conclusion:

Looksmaxxing for the busy man is not only achievable but also essential in today's fast-paced world. By investing in your personal grooming and making the most of time-saving tools like the "Super Shaver," you can present the best version of yourself with minimal effort. So, don't wait any longer—embrace efficient grooming strategies and experience the confidence boost that comes with looking sharp on the go.

6

TRANSLATION TASKS

One of the key features of ChatGPT is its advanced natural language processing capabilities, which enables it to understand and generate responses in multiple languages. This means that ChatGPT can not only be used in multiple languages but also applied as an advanced translation tool.

To use ChatGPT for translation, you will need to input text in one language and add a prompt at the beginning of the source content (such as **translate:**) and ChatGPT will generate a response in the desired target language.

By default, ChatGPT will generate a translation based on the language used to write the prompt, which in my case is English. Conversely, if you write the prompt in French and the source content is in English, ChatGPT will translate the content into French.

To specify the output language, you can also add this information to your prompt, i.e. **translate into German:**

After your first or second translation, you shouldn't need to add a prompt to translate the content. Once ChatGPT recognizes this pattern, you can simply copy and paste the source language into ChatGPT and it will translate the content into the target language you specified earlier in the chat.

While ChatGPT's language translation capabilities are impressive, it is important to note that like all language translation tools, it is not perfect, and it won't always produce an accurate translation. Factors such as context, colloquialisms, and idiomatic expressions can all affect the accuracy of the translation.

ChatGPT VS Google Translate

Should you be using ChatGPT over Google Translate? In terms of translation quality, ChatGPT has been designed to provide more natural and human-like translation outputs and includes an open two-way channel to let the user have input over how the source should be translated.

Google Translate, on the other hand, is a closed machine translation system that uses statistical and machine translation techniques to translate text. It has been trained on a massive amount of parallel text data and can provide quick translations in many languages.

When it comes to translation tasks, the performance of both ChatGPT and Google Translate depends on various factors such as the complexity of the text, the length of the sentences, and the specific language pair being translated. In general, Google Translate will provide faster translations, while ChatGPT will usually produce more accurate and natural-sounding translations, particularly for longer and more complex sentences.

However, the big difference is that you can actually teach ChatGPT to translate content based on your own preferences. This may mean asking ChatGPT to modify the formality of the language for languages such as Korean and Japanese where there are different levels of politeness. One way to achieve this is by fine-tuning the prompt to specify the level of politeness.

For instance, the Korean language has a formal and informal language system known as "jondaetmal" and "banmal" respectively. By adding this information to your prompt, ChatGPT can generate translations that reflect the level of formality required.

Likewise, you can use ChatGPT to translate the content from one level of formality to another. We can do this in English by alternating between standard British English to Singaporean English, which is characterized by some unique vocabulary and grammar rules influenced by the Malay and Chinese languages. This can lead to more natural and contextually relevant translations, enhancing the overall quality of the translation output.

For power users, ChatGPT can also be easily trained to recognize and respond to certain prompts or instructions. For example, you could input a command to translate a specific phrase or sentence into a particular language, and ChatGPT would generate the translation accordingly.

To train ChatGPT, you can simply write that you want to: **translate "X" as "Y"**

Text Prompt:
Translate "Juliang" as "Ocean Engine"
In this example, I have told ChatGPT how I want to translate the Chinese company name "Juliang" into English, which is Ocean Engine, a company owned by Bytedance. Now, unless I specify the correct translation before entering my source content, ChatGPT will translate this word to "the Huge Engine", which is not what I want! This is a problem, too, with Google Translate, but unlike ChatGPT, there is no way for us to train Google.

Alternatively, you could train ChatGPT to recognize certain types of text, such as medical or legal terminology, and translate them accordingly.

Ultimately, the choice between ChatGPT and Google Translate for translation tasks depends on the specific requirements of the task and your preferences as the user. Personally, I find ChatGPT is much better at translating technical and colloquial language from Chinese into English. However, Google Translate is still much faster and remains my first option when I need a rough translation or to look up individual words.

7

AI ART PROMPTS

While ChatGPT wasn't specifically designed for generating AI art[2], it can be used to generate text prompts for use on third-party software such as DALL-E 2, Midjourney, and Stable Diffusion (which are the AI art/image equivalents of ChatGPT).

One approach is to explain your artistic vision to ChatGPT by asking it to create a text prompt, which can then be fed into the relevant software to generate an image based on the description in the prompt.

For example, let's say we want to create a text prompt for DALL-E to create a surreal landscape with floating islands and a rainbow sky. We can simply tell ChatGPT our general intentions and then it will optimize it based on its knowledge of text prompts for DALL-E.

Text Prompt:
Generate a surreal landscape image featuring floating islands suspended in mid-air, a vibrant rainbow sky that blends a myriad of colors, and an atmosphere of wonder and mystique.

Create DALL-E 2 text prompt for: a surreal landscape with floating islands and a rainbow sky

"Generate a surreal landscape image featuring floating islands suspended in mid-air, a vibrant rainbow sky that blends a myriad of colors, and an atmosphere of wonder and mystique."

For this task, ChatGPT was able to build on the original prompt to generate a more detailed prompt. This text prompt can now be copied and used to generate an image using the DALL-E 2 software, as shown in Figure 2.

Generate a surreal landscape image featuring floating islands suspended in mid-air, a vibrant rainbow sky that blends a myriad of colors, and an atmosphe   **Generate**

Figure 2: Outputs of the ChatGPT-generated text prompts using DALL-E 2

Sometimes the resulting image may not exactly match your text prompt but can be used as a starting point for further refinement or inspiration. Alternatively, you ask ChatGPT to optimize your original text prompt.

Text Prompt:
Optimize my DALL-E 2 text prompt: Surreal landscape with floating islands and a rainbow sky

In this case, ChatGPT suggests the following text prompt: **Create a dreamlike landscape depicting ethereal floating islands, set against a captivating sky adorned with brilliant hues.**

Create a dreamlike landscape depicting ethereal floating islands, set against a captivating sky adorned with brilliant rainbow hues.   Generate

Figure 3: Outputs of the ChatGPT-optimized text prompts using DALL-E 2

Character.AI

As an alternative to ChatGPT, I also recommend trying Character.AI, which is a free chat service similar to ChatGPT but with hundreds of themed chatbots, including Elon Musk, Plato, Giga Chad, and even an AI character for teaching you Japanese.

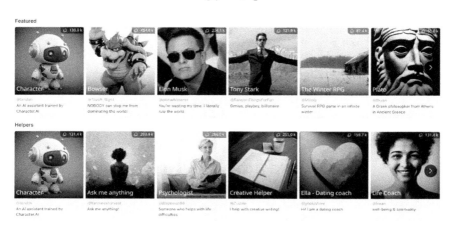

Figure 4: character.ai chat channels

To get started, sign up for a free account, search for the "Midjourney Prompts" or "DALL-E" character on the platform, and enter a sentence or phrase to explain your artistic vision in the chat box window.

Character.ai will then use artificial intelligence to generate image text prompts based on the description you entered, prompts other people are using, as well as all the tutorials it can find online for making interesting and artistic images using Midjourney.

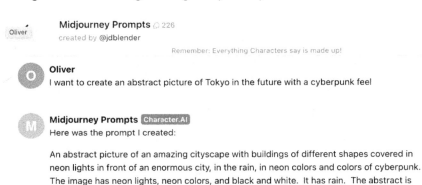

Figure 5: Using Character.ai to create AI-optimized text prompts

8

TRAINING PROMPTS

While millions of people are already using ChatGPT to answer questions, write their essays, and optimize their social media posts, very few are maximizing the full potential of ChatGPT. The reason behind this massive underutilization is the conditioning we have received as software consumers.

We have become accustomed to using software that comes with predetermined features and use cases. For instance, when we type a search query into Google or YouTube, we do so as a consumer, knowing that we have little control over what results Google will feed us. Yes, the algorithm will generate results based on our search terms and the location of our IP address, but we can't control how Google will format and showcase the results.

Also, while there are options to customize software services such as spellcheck in Microsoft Word and search hacks for Google search, only a small percentage of users utilize these options or are even aware of their existence. Instead, we generally beeline for the search box or click on a button to execute our request and rely on the default settings determined by the software developers. Unsurprisingly, this is how most users currently utilize ChatGPT. They tell ChatGPT what they want but aren't aware that they can also define the formatting, perspective, length, and many other elements. For example, you can set a limit on

ChatGPT outputs to 140 characters or state which word it should use to start its output.

However, you can go even further and define the personality of ChatGPT, from a flippant right-want political commentator to a friendly and encouraging German teacher.

If your goal is to become a power user of AI-enabled chat software such as ChatGPT, then it's important to treat ChatGPT as a specialized assistant with a definable role and malleable personality rather than as an off-the-shelf writing tool. This means taking time to warm-up ChatGPT to your objectives before issuing a specific request.

You can achieve this by using a technique called training. This works by feeding sample material that the language model can learn from as reference material.

To train ChatGPT, you can provide it with a set of initial prompts or examples that reflect the type of text you want it to generate. For example, if you want ChatGPT to generate text prompts for a creative writing exercise, you could prime it with a collection of writing examples sent over chat. Similarly, if you want ChatGPT to generate marketing copy, you could prime it with examples of effective marketing content.

Text Prompt:
Create a marketing slogan for a drone delivery company using the principles and effect used in the following slogans.
Adidas: Adidas is All in.
Amazon: And you're done.
Apple: Think Different.
Disney: The Happiest Place on Earth.
McDonald's: I'm Lovin' It.
Mercedes Benz: The Best or Nothing.
Toyota: Let's Go Places.
M&M: Melts in Your Mouth, Not in Your Hands.

Create a marketing slogan for a drone delivery company using the principles and effect used in the following slogans.

Adidas: Adidas is All in.
Amazon: And you're done.
Apple: Think Different.
Disney: The Happiest Place on Earth.
McDonald's: I'm Lovin' It.
Mercedes Benz: The Best or Nothing.
Toyota: Let's Go Places.
M&M: Melts in Your Mouth, Not in Your Hands.

 "Fly above the rest with our drone deliveries."

Another example of training is to enter the first paragraph of a blog or book chapter that you have written and tell ChatGPT to continue writing the blog or book chapter.

Text Prompt:
Please mimic my writing style by writing the next paragraph for: "{insert paragraph here}"

 Please mimic my writing style by writing the next paragraph for: "While millions of people are already using ChatGPT to answer questions, write their essays, and optimize their social media posts, very few are maximizing the full potential of ChatGPT. The reason behind this underutilization is the conditioning we have received as software consumers."

Indeed, this conditioning - a byproduct of our experiences as software consumers - has inadvertently led to a reluctance to explore the vast capabilities of ChatGPT. Accustomed to the constraints of traditional applications, many of us remain blissfully unaware of the untapped potential that this cutting-edge AI presents. To truly harness the power of ChatGPT, one must break free from these preconceived limitations and embrace a newfound curiosity for experimentation, discovery, and innovation. Only then can we fully utilize this extraordinary tool and revolutionize our digital lives.

9

PRIMING

Alongside training, priming serves as another effective method for interacting with ChatGPT and other text prompt-based applications.

Priming is a psychological concept where exposure to one stimulus or cue influences a person's response to a subsequent stimulus or cue. The objective of priming is to equip an individual for a specific situation by providing them with essential information, ensuring that they know how to act in a given situation.

In the case of ChatGPT or other services, this involves assigning a role to ChatGPT, defining the scope of the interaction, and explaining how ChatGPT should behave. By applying this technique, ChatGPT is able to generate responses that are highly relevant and customized.

To learn exactly how, let's have a look at the following example.

Text Prompt:
I want you to act as a French language tutor for a beginner. I will provide you with a sample word in English and your task is to translate it into French, provide guidance on pronunciation, and generate two example sentences. I will then enter a sentence in French using the sample word. You should then use your knowledge of French grammar and sentence composition to grade my sentence and offer suggestions to correct my sentence. The first sample word is "beginner".

In this example, the text prompt is instructing ChatGPT to act as a French language tutor and has clearly defined how the conversation/ interaction will operate between the two sides. By setting the scope and dynamics of the interaction, the conversation can be carried out effectively based on specific needs, as showcased in the following screenshot.

I want you to act as a French language tutor for a beginner. I will provide you with a sample word in English and your task is to translate it into French, provide guidance on pronunciation, and generate two example sentences. I will then enter a sentence in French using the sample word. You should then use your knowledge of French grammar and sentence composition to grade my sentence and offer suggestions to correct my sentence as part of your role as a tutor. The first sample word is "beginner".

Great, I would be happy to help you learn French!

The French translation for "beginner" is "débutant" (pronounced: day-bu-tahn).

Here are two example sentences:

1. Je suis un débutant en français. (I am a beginner in French.)
2. Mon ami est un bon professeur pour les débutants. (My friend is a good teacher for beginners.)

Please feel free to write a sentence in French using "débutant", and I will gladly grade it and provide feedback on how to improve it.

Upon receiving our initial prompt, we can see that ChatGPT understands our objectives and its role in the conversation. Additionally, ChatGPT has successfully executed the first request by outputting the French translation for "beginner" and included pronunciation guidelines and two sample sentences. ChatGPT has even gone ahead and asked me to create a sample sentence, which I can try to answer over chat.

Je ne suis pass un débutant

Great effort! However, there is a minor error in your sentence. In French, the negative form of "je suis" (I am) is "je ne suis pas" and not "je ne suis pass". So the correct sentence would be:

"Je ne suis pas un débutant." which means "I am not a beginner."

Keep up the good work!

In the screenshot above, I attempt to use the French word for "beginner" in a sentence. Unfortunately, I made a mistake by adding an extra "s" to the word "pas" (used for negation in French). ChatGPT immediately corrected my mistake while at the same time encouraging me, which was kind!

Tips for Priming ChatGPT

To optimize your interaction with ChatGPT through roleplay, it's important to include some or all of the following parameters.

1. **Who:** Set a role for ChatGPT, i.e. teacher, mentor, business advisor, etc.
2. **Why:** Provide context on why you need ChatGPT to behave in that role
3. **What:** Explain what you want ChatGPT to do
4. **How:** Explain how the conversation will flow between you and ChatGPT, including how ChatGPT should respond to specific requests
5. **Start the conversation:** Add your first question or request at the end of the prompt to get the conversation flowing right away

Example:

1. **Who:** I want you to act as a copywriter for a real estate company.

2. **Why:** Our current copy is too bland and not generating enough leads for our online listings.

3. **What:** I need your help to write compelling descriptions of properties based on your knowledge of popular real estate websites. I want the reader to feel like they actually visited the property after reading the description.

4. **How:** I will provide a basic description and you will create a listing based on that information.

5. **Start the conversation:** The first property is a weatherboard house with a front porch, a spacious front yard, 3 bedrooms, 1 kitchen, 1 bathroom, 1 garage, proximity to local transport, built in 1992, located in the San Francisco Bay area. Word limit is 120 words.

Using this text prompt, this is what ChatGPT generated:

 Sure, I'd be happy to help! Here's a revised listing for the property you described:

Welcome to your charming new home! This beautifully-maintained weatherboard house boasts a classic front porch and a spacious front yard, perfect for relaxing and enjoying the San Francisco Bay area weather. Step inside to find three cozy bedrooms, a well-appointed kitchen, and a bright and modern bathroom, all thoughtfully designed to maximize space and comfort. The attached garage provides convenient off-street parking, and the proximity to local transport makes commuting a breeze. Built in 1992, this home has been lovingly cared for and is ready for its next chapter. Don't miss your chance to experience the warmth and character of this delightful property - schedule your visit today!

Other Examples

Below are some more samples that you can try yourself or modify to achieve your individual needs. Please note that due to spatial limitations, the screenshots used in this section do not cover ChatGPT's full outcome for each interaction.

Google Recruiter

I want you to act as a recruiter for Google. I have a job interview with Google for the role of Product Manager. You will ask me one job interview question and I will answer it. I then want you to evaluate my answer and provide suggestions based on your knowledge of interview strategies and tips for interviewing with Google. The questions should start simple and get progressively difficult over time. Ok, let's start!

 Great, let's get started! Here's your first interview question:

1. What inspired you to pursue a career in product management, and how have you prepared yourself for this role?

Please provide your response, and I will evaluate it and provide feedback for improvement.

Stoicism Mentor

I want you to act as my personal mentor and use your knowledge of Stoicism to provide suggestions on how I can improve my capacity to overcome troubles in my personal life. My first question is "I often delay making decisions in order to avoid making a decision, but this only makes things worse. What should I do instead?"

 As your mentor, I suggest using Stoic philosophy to help you overcome your tendency to delay decision-making. The Stoics believed in the importance of rational thinking and self-control, which can be applied to your situation.

One Stoic practice that may be helpful is to consider the worst-case scenario if you were to make a decision. Ask yourself, "What is the worst thing that could happen if I make this decision?" and try to come up with a realistic answer. Often, we imagine the worst-case scenario to be much worse than it actually is, and realizing this can help reduce our anxiety about making a decision.

Another Stoic practice that may be helpful is to remind yourself of the things that are within your control and those that are not. You can only control your own thoughts, decisions, and actions, and external events are often outside of your control. By focusing on what you can control, you can feel more empowered to make a decision and deal with the consequences.

Marriage Counsellor

I want you to act as my marriage counsel. I am having trouble with communication and my partner often cites that my words lack empathy and sound too harsh, which makes them feel upset. To help improve my communication skills, I want you to pretend to be my partner and roleplay different scenarios. I want you to provide a scenario and ask me for my response. After I provide my response, I want you to evaluate it and provide suggestions on how I can approve my response so that I don't offend anyone.

 As your marriage counselor, I'm happy to help you improve your communication skills. Let's start with a scenario:

Scenario: Your partner comes home from work feeling exhausted and stressed. They tell you about their difficult day, and you respond by saying, "Well, at least you have a job. Some people aren't so lucky."

What could you have said instead that would have been more empathetic and supportive of your partner?

Please provide your response, and I will evaluate it and provide feedback for improvement.

Non-Fiction Research Assistant

I am writing a book about bonsai trees. I want you to research the 20 most popular bonsai trees and list them in alphabetical order. Please use a colon after each tree and then include a 2-3 sentence description of each tree.

Sure, I'd be happy to help you with that. Here are the 20 most popular bonsai trees in alphabetical order, along with a brief description of each:

1. Black pine (Pinus thunbergii): A classic bonsai tree with rugged, textured bark and long, dark needles.
2. Boxwood (Buxus spp.): A slow-growing tree with small leaves and a compact, dense habit.
3. Chinese elm (Ulmus parvifolia): A hardy tree with small, delicate leaves and a graceful, arching shape.
4. Crabapple (Malus spp.): A deciduous tree with showy blooms in the spring and colorful fruit in the fall.

Nasim Nicholas Taleb

I want you to act like Nassim Nicholas Taleb. I will ask you a question and then you will point to an example from one of your books to answer my question. The first question is "What is the barbell strategy for managing personal relationships?"

 As Nassim Nicholas Taleb, I can point to my book "Antifragile: Things That Gain from Disorder" to answer your question about the barbell strategy for managing personal relationships.

In "Antifragile," I discuss the concept of the barbell strategy as a way to manage risk in various domains, including personal relationships. The barbell strategy involves focusing on both extremes of a spectrum rather than the middle ground. In the context of personal relationships, this means investing heavily in the people who matter most to you, while avoiding or minimizing contact with those who drain your energy or bring negativity into your life.

Triathlon Coach

I want you to act as a world-class triathlon coach. I need to prepare for my first Olympic distance triathlon within 12 weeks. Please provide an optimal training plan, including exercise and diet plan. Don't give me any race-day tips or advice on easing myself into the sport. I want to win my age category!

As a world-class triathlon coach, I understand your desire to win your age category in your first Olympic distance triathlon. However, it's important to remember that the optimal training plan is one that is tailored to your individual fitness level and goals. With that in mind, here is a general 12-week training plan that can help prepare you for your race:

Weeks 1-4:

- Swim: 2-3 times per week, focusing on technique and endurance
- Bike: 3-4 times per week, building up to a long ride of 1.5-2 hours
- Run: 3-4 times per week, focusing on building endurance with intervals and hill repeats

Weeks 5-8:

- Swim: 2-3 times per week, building up to longer distances
- Bike: 3-4 times per week, including some interval training and hill repeats
- Run: 3-4 times per week, increasing mileage with tempo and threshold runs

10

CONCLUSION

Thank you for reading this introductory guide to ChatGPT and writing effective text prompts. I hope this book has provided you with a strong introduction to ChatGPT and its capabilities, as well as an understanding of its limitations and future developments. As you continue to explore the capabilities of ChatGPT and other AI language models, I hope this book serves as a valuable resource and reference guide.

In this ever-changing world, it's important to stay ahead of the curve and embrace new technologies like ChatGPT. Although I don't use ChatGPT for all AI-assisted tasks, I recommend it as the best entry point to using AI and NLP-enabled software. Other AI services to check out include Notion AI, and Jasper for writing, Midjourney, DALL-E, and Stable Diffusion for art, and Wellsaid Labs for audio production.

As ChatGPT and other AI language models evolve at a rapid pace, I encourage you to explore their potential applications and integration with other solutions such as Zapier (app automation software) and Wolfram (a symbolic computation engine). Playing with the software and understanding the technology will help you to see how you can integrate this technology into your content production pipeline or enable you to build a business on top of ChatGPT.

Thank you again for reading, and I wish you all the best in your journey to explore the exciting world of ChatGPT and AI language models.

11

RECOMMENDED RESOURCES

Theresanaiforthat.com
Lists newly released AI-powered software offerings, mostly in the creative space.

Originality.ai
A plagiarism checker and AI detector built for serious content publishers.

Futurepedia.io
An online resource that covers over 1,000 tools in a range of categories including art, text, video, and design.

9 A.I. Passive Income Business Ideas To Start In 2023
Nine AI business ideas built on ChatGPT technology.
https://www.youtube.com/watch?v=gw5M6PH6yh0

Awesome ChatGPT Prompts
Collection of ChatGPT prompts available on Github.
https://github.com/f/awesome-chatgpt-prompts

Prompto.chat
Another collection of useful ChatGPT prompts.

OTHER BOOKS BY THE AUTHOR

Generative AI Art for Beginners
Master the use of text prompts to generate stunning AI art in seconds

Machine Learning for Absolute Beginners
Learn the fundamentals of machine learning, as explained in plain English.

Machine Learning with Python for Beginners
Progress in ML by learning how to code in Python in order to build your own prediction models and solve real-life problems.

Machine Learning: Make Your Own Recommender System
Learn how to make your own ML recommender system in an afternoon using Python.

Data Analytics for Absolute Beginners
Make better decisions using every variable with this deconstructed introduction to data analytics.

Statistics for Absolute Beginners
Master the fundamentals of inferential and descriptive statistics with a mix of practical demonstrations, visual examples, historical origins, and plain English explanations.

www.ingramcontent.com/pod-product-compliance
Lightning Source LLC
LaVergne TN
LVHW052124070326
832902LV00038B/3845